WHAT YOU SHOULD KNOW ABOUT

GETTING ALONG

WITH A

NEW PARENT

WHAT YOU SHOULD KNOW ABOUT

GETTING ALONG

WITH A

NEW PARENT

WILLIAM L. COLEMAN

Augsburg
MINNEAPOLIS

WHAT YOU SHOULD KNOW ABOUT GETTING ALONG WITH A NEW
PARENT

Cover design: Bob Fuller
Interior design: Jim Brisson

Library of Congress Cataloging-in-Publication Data

Coleman, William L.
    What you should know about getting along with a new parent /
William L. Coleman.
        p.   cm.
    Summary: Discusses some of the situations and feelings that can
cause problems in stepfamilies and how to deal with them in a
loving, Christian way.
    ISBN 0-8066-2611-9 :
    1. Stepchildren—Juvenile literature.   2. Stepparents—Juvenile
literature.   3. Stepchildren—Religious life—Juvenile literature.
[1. Stepfamilies.   2. Interpersonal relations.   3. Christian life.]
I. Title.
HQ777.7.C65   1992
306.874—dc20   92-18335
                                                          CIP
                                                          AC

The paper used in this publication meets the minimum requirements of
American National Standard for Information Sciences—Permanence of
Paper for Printed Library Materials, ANSI Z329.48-1984.   ∞™

Manufactured in U.S.A.   AF 9-2611

96   95   94   93   92   1   2   3   4   5   6   7   8   9   10

CONTENTS

CONTENTS

CONTENTS

CONTENTS

ACKNOWLEDGMENTS

Even though I had a stepmother, there was much more I needed to learn about stepfamilies. A number of individuals and groups were generous in sharing their experiences and knowledge.

I particularly want to thank Connie Chambers of Stepfamily Association of America, Inc. She gave me a practical interview and extended guidance. I also appreciate the Lincoln, Nebraska, support group of that association for sharing their experiences with me. In consideration of the people who shared with me, I have not used any of the actual stories I heard.

Cliff Switzer, a stepfather, was also a tremendous help in showing the bright side of stepfamilies.

◆ ◆ ◆ ◆ ◆

Suggestions for Adults

Helping a troubled child is a kind and caring act. Anything you can do to help stabilize a child in a tumultuous world is a loving contribution. This book is intended to encourage you in the task of mending a child's heart and soul.

It is difficult enough for children to have to sift through a confusing world. The added turmoil of a traumatized family plus the rebuilding of a new family frequently becomes an emotional overload. That is why a child needs an understanding person who can help him or her to calm down and think through the difficulties. We see Christ doing this when he gathers the children into his lap and blesses them.

Children in stepfamilies face enormous issues. Questions of love, discipline, jealousy, abandonment, and reassurance are heavy on their hearts. If they look to traditional families to find the answers, they will only be bewildered, because stepfamilies are different. Stepfamilies may have great strengths, but they are not biological families. We only hurt children if we expect them to pretend that nothing has happened.

This book has many uses for both children and adults. The following guidelines will help the reader to get the most out of it.

11

1. *Read this book together.* Ideally an adult will share this material with a child. One-on-one contact allows for reaction and response. If sharing is impractical, certainly leave a copy with the child.
2. *Take your time.* A chapter or two at a time could be the most effective. Start at the first chapter, but move willingly to any topic that seems urgent or compelling to the child.
3. *Don't assume that you know what the child is thinking.* Stepparenting is mysterious: it is not just a matter of who lives at whose house in a numerical or technical sense. Beneath that are emotional reactions, some of which may be peculiar to an individual.
4. *Raise questions.* Avoid using probing or interrogating questions. Instead, ask open-ended questions that raise issues, and then allow the child to phrase the responses. Don't conduct a quiz. Broad questions are more likely to get a relaxed reaction.
5. *Don't play games of deception.* Stepparenting is often a puzzle to the child; don't add to the confusion. Be honest and straightforward but not harsh or crude. Life can be like shifting sand for the child, and he or she needs a stable, dependable person.

6. *Don't try to protect people.* If a family member is acting in a terrible fashion, don't try to defend the person. Raise questions but let the child make his or her own evaluation. We fall into a trap when we attempt to whitewash the behavior of others.
7. *Be positive.* "Ain't it awful" becomes tiresome. Point gently and genuinely to every good part of stepparenting that occurs.
8. *Remind the child of the good parts.* All of us forget. Don't tire of reinforcing the strengths, joys, and hope. Constantly remind the child of the love, acceptance, and forgiveness God gives through Jesus.

May God bless you as you touch a young life in a healing process.

◆ ◆ ◆ ◆ ◆

The Big Adventure

Some people have to travel to South American jungles or climb mountain peaks to find exciting challenges. Members of stepfamilies have plenty of adventure in their own backyard.

What interesting things does your stepparent like to do? How can you help a new stepsister or stepbrother fit in at home or at school? Are there any fascinating stepparents that come along with this change? Does your stepparent camp, or do woodwork, or play ball, or like to travel, or shoot pool? Look at a stepparent as an unopened treasure chest.

Stepfamilies can be eventful and even amazing. May God give your family a great today and a better tomorrow.

Bill Coleman

◆ ◆ ◆ ◆ ◆

Why You?

Have you ever watched a television comedy where everyone in the family seems to get along? When the mom and dad get angry it is a kidding kind of anger, and they always make up by the end of the show. The children tease each other, but it's usually low-key, and no one ever acts mean or holds a grudge.

Do you wonder why you don't have a neat little family like that?

Have you ever sat in school and listened to a friend describe his or her family vacation? Did he or she talk about singing around a campfire or hiking through the woods with Mom and Dad bouncing cheerfully along? They sound like the ideal family where everyone gets along great.

Do you wonder why you don't have a neat little family like that?

If you are like most people, you sometimes feel sorry for yourself. When a family splits and another group of individuals tries to blend in as a new family, there are a number of disappointments. Sometimes you wish and you dream that it could have been another way, but it isn't. Someone moved away or died or something happened to cause a miserable split.

You had nothing to do with causing that split, but you have to suffer from it. There isn't anything fair about it. But it happened, and your life is affected.

Why you? There is no good answer to that question. Why do some people get cancer? Why do others get into car accidents? Why do some parents lose their jobs? Why do tornadoes hit some houses and miss others?

The family you once knew is no more, and a new family has come about in your world. These are the facts, and you probably had almost no say about it. But now you have a great deal to say and do. You can decide to pout and feel sorry for yourself as some children do. They make themselves miserable, and they make the people around them fairly uncomfortable, too. Or you can cheer up and make the most of the situation. Look for ways to enjoy your new family. Those who give themselves a good attitude seem to enjoy life the most.

If you feel brokenhearted because of what has happened to your family, ask God to help you have a better attitude. God is interested in people who have had terrible disappointments. God won't do all the work in changing your outlook, but God will help heal a broken heart: "He heals the brokenhearted and binds up their wounds" (Psalm 147:3).

◆ ◆ ◆ ◆ ◆

What Do You Tell
a Friend?

Families change. Children grow up and leave home. A grandparent dies, and the other one might remarry. Parents sometimes get divorced and remarried. Some families change slowly, while others frequently have new people coming in or going out.

Change happens so often that probably at least half of the students in your class have divorced and remarried parents. It isn't uncommon. People won't be shocked to know that your family is unsettled and is suffering from some shifting around.

There is no need to be embarrassed or to feel ashamed because your parents are getting new partners. That's their decision. Their decision certainly affects you, but you can't control the behavior of adults.

Even though you know all of that, it is still awkward to have a changing family. What do you say to your friends? If your dad has moved out, or your stepfather has a different last name than you, or there are some new kids living at your house, you might feel the need to explain to your friends.

A simple, straightforward explanation is the best thing to offer a puzzled friend: "My dad moved out." "My mom is remarrying this guy named Syd." "I've got a new stepbrother living with us."

This will help your friends understand why someone is missing from your house or why someone has been added. Anything else you might explain is up to you.

Don't make up excuses for what has happened to your family. Tell your friends the facts. Otherwise they might worry or be afraid for you. If they ask for more information, you decide how much you want to say. The simple facts will be enough for most friends.

Be a Child Again

If you lived with only one parent for a while, probably a great deal was expected of you. Maybe your mother said, "You will have to be the man around here," or your dad said, "You need to take responsibility for the house now." That's a lot of pressure on a fourth, fifth, or sixth grader.

But you probably jumped in and helped out. Sometimes you had to listen to your single parent complain about money, work, loneliness, and maybe even about your other parent.

Those were tough times, but mostly you held up well and pitched in. You had broad shoulders for your parent to lean on.

Now things have improved. Your mom or dad has remarried and, while that takes some adjusting, your parent has another person to help carry the load.

But the change has been hard. It was almost as if one day you were a child and the next day you were an adult. Now your parent has remarried, and you aren't sure who you are anymore.

Children are special people, and they can remain children for only a little while. Why not go back and finish being a child. (Not a baby, because you certainly aren't that!) Let the adults worry about paying the electric bill. Let the adults worry about getting the car fixed or finding a plumber. Adults usually handle those things rather well.

Go back now. Get a ball and a bat, a video game, a pet frog, a doll named Angie. You have unfinished business. You need to complete your childhood before it gets away.

It's great to be a child. That's why Jesus loves children. They are fresh, trusting, playful, and imaginative, and usually they love life.

You don't want to stay a child forever, but neither do you want to miss it. Now that your parents seem a little more stable, find something that children like to do.

"Jesus said, 'Let the little children come to me, and do not hinder them, for the kingdom of heaven belongs to such as these' " (Matthew 19:14).

◆ ◆ ◆ ◆ ◆

Two Sets of Rules

At your father's house you watch television while you eat. But at your mother's house the set stays off until after the dishes are done.

Your mother lets you stay up until eleven o'clock. Your father wants the lights out by ten.

Dad never hassles you about cleaning up your room. Mom won't let you go outside until everything is in the right place.

Your mother doesn't correct your English. If you say "ain't" at your father's place, you get your head chewed off.

There are two sets of rules. One for House A and another for House B. Sometimes you may want to compare the two and complain a lot. By griping, you can fail to enjoy living at either house.

When you go to school, you follow a set of rules. Those rules may be different than the ones at home. But you can get along very well under two sets of rules.

Think about it: You behave one way at church, another way on the playground. You lie in the sun on the beach, but you don't lie down on the floor at the mall. You eat popcorn at the movies, but you don't eat popcorn at piano recitals. You eat with your fingers on camping trips, but you use knives and forks at home.

If one parent has one set of rules and the other parent has a different set of rules, both parents might be correct. House A and House B may not be the same, yet both may be good places to stay.

Smart people make the adjustments and enjoy staying at each house.

A Parent Who Has Died

Not all children who have a stepparent have one because their parents got a divorce. Some might have a stepparent because their mother or father died. If that is what has happened in your family, you know how much you miss your mom or dad. You can close your eyes and the memories and pictures all come back. You know what it's like to be lonely.

You also know that the stepparent who has entered your life cannot take the place of the one who died no matter how good that new person is. No one will ever be like the parent you lost.

In some families, friction starts between the stepparent and the stepchild because the stepchild compares his or her dead parent with the stepparent. Often without thinking the child will say things like:

"My mother never made us go to bed."

"My father never yelled at us."

"My mother was a lot better cook."

"My father would have coached a ball team."

"My mother kept a cleaner house."

"My father took me for rides."

Most parents who have died were good people, but they weren't perfect. Sometimes children forget that.

It's good to talk about a parent who has died. That person meant a great deal to you, and you miss him or her tremendously. Your living parent must miss him or her, too.

But it isn't helpful to compare people. Each person has his or her own good qualities. Remember to be kind to your stepparent.

◆ ◆ ◆ ◆ ◆

Hansel and Gretel
Stuck Together

You have probably heard the old German fairy tale about a brother and sister who get a wicked stepmother. Since food is scarce, the stepmother convinces the father to lose the children, Hansel and Gretel, in the woods.

The brother and sister hear that they are to be abandoned, and they leave bread crumbs along the path so they can find their way back home. Unfortunately, birds eat the crumbs, and the children become lost. Hansel and Gretel find themselves at a gingerbread house where they encounter a wicked witch who plans to eat them.

After many twists and turns, the children finally make their way home again. They discover that the stepmother has died, and they live happily with their father.

Sometimes Hansel is the hero, and at other times it is his sister, Gretel, who shows great courage. As brother and sister they draw close and depend on each other. They eat candy from the gingerbread house, rescue one another, and take turns riding across the river on the back of a white duck.

Fairy tales like this give stepmothers a bad name. In the real world, most children have kind and loving stepmothers. Most stepmothers are sacrificial, helpful, and thoughtful adults.

But the story of Hansel and Gretel offers something positive, too. The good part of the story is that a brother and sister, under terrible stress, chose to help each other. Hansel and Gretel could have fought and bickered and made life extra hard for themselves. Instead they looked out for each other and came through some terribly tough times together.

With so much change going on, we all need someone to lean on once in a while. Too often children want to stay away from their "icky" sister or their "creepy" brother, but it's also nice to know she or he cares.

When you feel lonely, confused, or hurt and need someone to talk to, take a quick look around. Often brothers or sisters are exactly the right persons who will listen to you. Whether they are younger or older, chances are they understand what you are going through. After all, they live there, too.

Maybe they can give you some advice about what to do. Maybe they can just listen. You may not be looking for advice; you may just want someone to hear how you feel.

Good friends are hard to find. It's a good idea not to ignore brothers or sisters just because they are brothers or sisters.

◆ ◆ ◆ ◆ ◆

Sharing Stuff

Fish can be just as territorial as wolves, chee-tahs, or gibbons. Cichlid are fish that fight their neighbors to keep intruders from swimming in their part of the water. The male cichlid will bump into other fish or swish water at visitors by tossing its tail around.

If the cichlid's gentle tactics fail to frighten the other fish off, he may resort to force. He bites the upper jaw of an intruding fish, which usually sends the newcomer scurrying away.

In some ways people are territorial, too. We like our space, and that's fine. Privacy is good for most of us, but privacy can go too far and turn into simple selfishness.

Hoarding the remote control, refusing to share a basketball, fighting over a chair, and hog-ging a headset can be territorial acts that lead to family war. Before long, who knows, you may start biting each other on the upper lip to show who's boss.

Living with people means sharing stuff: raincoats, hats, airplane glue, and fingernail pol-ish. Hair dryers, video games, footballs, and base-ball bats, too. Politeness is important. We all like to be asked, and "please" is a beautiful word. But fighting over turf just leads to more fighting.

The Bible teaches us this great principle: "Do not forget to do good and to share with others, for with such sacrifices God is pleased" (Hebrews 13:16).

What stuff do you have that someone else would enjoy using? Why not surprise that person by offering it to him or her? Share your tapes, your belt, your sunglasses, your windbreaker, your guitar, or your skateboard.

When we share we make everybody smile, including God.

◆ ◆ ◆ ◆ ◆

Making a "th" Sound

Place your tongue on your two front teeth and practice making a "th" sound. People who learn English as a second language say this is a hard sound to make, but with practice it can be learned.

After the tongue is placed on the front teeth, blow air out to push your tongue away from the teeth. It is a gentle, rolling sound with a soft thickness to it, much like velvet.

Don't give up until this skill has been mastered. The "th" sound is necessary if you are going to say two of the most important words in the English language. The words "thank you" begin with a good strong "th."

When you were much younger, you probably said "tank you." Children and others learning the language do that because they push off too hard from their teeth. If you say "thank you" often, you will acquire just the right touch.

There are many people to whom you can practice saying "thank you." For starters, you can thank God, thank a teacher, thank a parent, and thank a stepparent.

In some families the stepparent is thanked less than anyone. But stepparents are often good listeners, are good advice givers, and are terrific at finding the right medicine in the cabinet.

Yet some stepparents very seldom hear the "th" sound. Their stepchildren see them daily, eat meals with them, and sometime seven ask them for help with homework. And too often the children forget to say "thank you."

The apostle Paul told Christians, "And be thankful" (Colossians 3:15b). People of all ages forget to show appreciation. But everyone likes to hear that "th" sound.

The Good Word Person

"You're going to be late for school, bone-head."

"Nice shoes. Are they your mother's?"

"Let me fix your collar. Can't you do anything right?"

"Your hat looks like a dead skunk."

"I've seen better looking legs on a cheap table."

Many people like to say "put-downs." That's the way they talk to their friends, their brothers, their sisters, even people they like the most. Often children intend a put-down as a sign that they think the person is special. Sometimes put-downs are funny, and a friend may respond with a put-down.

But, of course, put-downs are risky business. Occasionally someone misunderstands and feelings get hurt. We all know how miserable we feel when words hurt us.

Maybe you need to make an extra effort to say at least one good thing to each person in your family every day. That would take a little work but not much. Think of how you would feel if each person in your house gave you one sincere compliment each day.

"Your hair looks great this morning."

"Good job on those dishes last night."

"Boy, does your room look neat."

"Terrific job on that model."

"That was a special dessert last night."

"What a pretty sweater."

"Congratulations on your test."

We like to joke about each other, but if we joke all the time, it stops being funny. If we say exactly the right words at precisely the correct times, we can make people feel good about themselves.

"A man finds joy in giving an apt reply—and how good is a timely word!" (Proverbs 15:23).

The Change Game

When parents remarry, a flood of changes come rushing in. Children in the family may feel like they are on a small rowboat in a storm, getting tossed around, sometimes even afraid they might sink.

31

Every person is different. Not everyone sees the same changes; and of course, some changes are for the better while other changes really stink.

Let's be honest about the situation. Listed below are some areas in which changes *may* have occurred when your parent remarried. Not all of these areas are affected in every case, and there may be areas of change in your family that aren't listed here.

Go down the list and *react* to each word as you come to it. You might say things like "weird," "great," "terrific," "terrible," "a real bummer," or whatever. In some instances you might want to explain what you mean. That's up to you, of course.

Relax. Take your time and enjoy the exercise.

Home	Discipline
Money	Clothes
Food	Space
Family	Brothers and sisters
Communication	Friends
School	Stepparent
Parent (resident)	Parent (nonresident)
New rules	Church
Bedtime	Tension
Playfulness	Family conferences
Time together	Time alone

There is no way to win or lose at this game, but it might help you understand what you feel strongly about. It also could show what you think is not working well. If your reaction to some words was strong and unhappy, those are the ones you need to talk over.

Some of the words may have brought a smile to your face. In some situations you may be very thankful for the change. It is good to admit that, too.

◆ ◆ ◆ ◆ ◆

Two Kinds of Discipline

People who drive in the city have to be careful where they park. If they park in a "no parking" zone, they run the risk of getting a ticket or, worse yet, having their car towed away. That's inconvenient *and* expensive.

We are expected to have enough self-discipline to park in the correct place. If we lack self-control and park on the sidewalk or on someone's lawn or next to a fire hydrant, we get into trouble.

The dictionary gives several meanings for the word *discipline*. One of them is self-control. Another is punishment. You could say, either we discipline ourselves or someone else may discipline us.

Discipline isn't bad. It is absolutely necessary. Without discipline we might sleep half the day, never work, and let everything fall apart.

Sometimes children, just like adults who drive cars, refuse to discipline themselves. They might leave chewing gum on the sink or refuse to put the milk away. They might have a habit of leaving the front door open or letting their pet alligator run loose in the kitchen.

We have the first choice. Do we want to discipline or correct ourselves? Most of us don't like doing that *all* the time. Or we even forget to do what we should. Consequently we need someone else to help us control our actions, to lovingly teach us. Note that the word *punish* is not used. However, if someone disciplines us and we don't think he or she should, we often get angry. We don't like it if our brother tells us to eat our green beans. We don't like parents telling us either.

In stepfamilies one of the big questions is who should discipline the children and who should not. Should a stepparent discipline a stepchild? Discipline about what? How old is the child? How long have they known each other? How well do they get along? How many children are there in the family? Does everyone get disciplined alike, or are there favorites? Should only the natural parent discipline? That's too many questions. The answers to each may differ greatly from stepparent to stepparent.

Discipline is a good topic for a family conference. Everyone needs to sit down together and discuss who disciplines whom and under what circumstances. Even if you don't reach an agreement, at least you should understand how everyone feels.

Discipline is important, and how it is done is just as important. "No discipline seems pleasant at the time, but painful. Later on, however, it produces a harvest of righteousness and peace for those who are trained by it" (Hebrews 12:11).

Money Is a Big Deal

Joey needs a pair of tennis shoes, but his parents tell him that he will have to wait. The car is looking dumpy and doesn't want to start, but this isn't the time to spring for a new car. Laurie is going to get braces, and Mom says there might not be a vacation this year.

Does this sound like your family? Many families suffer at least some tension because of lack of money. There is no endless flow of money, and some things have to be put off. Other things will never be affordable. Even the people we sometimes envy because they have so many things worry about money.

In stepfamilies money is often a problem. Finances may not be a bigger deal than in other families, but it certainly seems that way. What makes it so terribly important? There are several stress factors when it comes to money and a stepfamily:

> *Child support.* A parent may not be paying child support on time or may not be paying it at all. That cuts down family income. Your stepparent might be paying child support to another family. That also cuts down on available money.
>
> *Alimony.* Your stepparent may need to send money regularly to a former spouse.
>
> *Gift buying.* The parent you live with may feel a need to get you an expensive birthday or Christmas present because he or she knows that your other parent will buy you expensive gifts. If they spend their money for presents, there will be less for everyday needs.
>
> *Bills for services.* A divorce may leave both families with added expenses. Parents might still be paying off lawyer fees, or family members may be seeing counselors. Sometimes the situation changes and parents go back to court. That becomes costly.
>
> *Start-up money.* After a divorce some families need to move to another house or buy an-

other car, and it's almost like starting all over again. Some parents go back to school. It costs money to make big adjustments.

If money seems like a big deal in your family, ask your parents what is happening. When we understand more of the total picture, we can usually handle things better. Stepfamilies may not have more financial problems than other families, but the money situation is worth talking about.

What to Call a Stepparent

When my father remarried, he said he would like me to call his new wife "Mother." Since I was a teenager at the time, and I didn't know her very well, I decided that would be too awkward for me. I could understand how my father felt about it, but he also needed to know my feelings and how I looked at my biological, or "natural," mother.

For some families this is never a problem. The first day some children get a new parent they will walk over and say, "Hi, Dad" or "Hi, Mom," and that takes care of it. But many children need some time to think it over and some time to become more comfortable with the stepparent before deciding what to call him or her.

Don't be too surprised if it changes over the years. Sometimes you may want to call a stepparent by his or her first name, and the next time you may want to use "Mom" or "Dad." One child I know always calls her stepmother by her first name except when she talks to someone else. Then she simply says, "My mom said she would help me sew it" or "My mom will give me a ride."

It's for the best when everyone can relax and not be too uptight over what people are called. What's more important may be the tone of voice and the meaning behind what we say. If we show respect between stepparent and stepchild, the exact name doesn't have to be such a huge deal. But sometimes it is a big deal, and the family has to work it out. Be sure and explain how you feel about what you should call your stepparent. Everyone should try to feel comfortable with it.

You shouldn't be forced to call someone a name you dislike. But neither should your stepparent be expected to put up with a name he or she doesn't want. This is where respect for each other really counts.

What would you like to be called? How does son or daughter or stepson or stepdaughter or just your first name sound? How do you want your stepparent to introduce you? Don't be touchy. It's best to say what you want.

Adults need to show respect for children, because children are people who have feelings. Likewise, children must have respect for adults because they are people, too. Whatever you agree to call each other, be big on respect.

"Show proper respect to everyone" (1 Peter 2:17a).

The Crowded Bathroom

Do you have a problem with your bathroom? Maybe someone is spending too much time in there before breakfast. Or perhaps another person leaves it a mess. He or she slops soap on the sink, piles towels on the floor, smashes the toothpaste in the middle, and leaves an ugly pile of hair in the drain.

Every morning you get upset at a bathroom that looks like a pig pen. Sometimes you might yell about it. Once or twice you complain to your parents. You might even scream at the person or persons who are responsible. Almost every day there is some hassle over the bathroom.

If this is the case, a family conference is in order.

Family conferences might be boring, and you might moan when you hear there is going to be one, but they can be great times to clear things up—even bathroom problems. A short discussion with everyone present could lead to some instant improvement. Good discussion is far better than hollering, door banging, getting even, and general chaos.

If you don't like calling it a family conference, call it something else. Think up a new name—maybe Security Council or Personnel Management or Family Club Meeting or whatever. Use a name that explains the purpose and suggests that good things could happen.

Either set a regular date for the family to meet or suggest how the group can be called together. Possibly anyone with a question, a problem, or a special announcement could call the family together right after you eat on Tuesday evenings or whenever best fits your family's schedule.

When a family has no way to meet and open a discussion, they have to find other ways to communicate. And some of those forms of communication don't do much to promote family unity.

Crowded bathrooms, borrowed clothing, broken promises, missing parts, unfair treatment, overloaded closets, and loud stereos can each be handled in a family setting. Sensible solutions can be shared, and the family can remain on friendly terms. Plus, the noise level around the house is a few decibels lower!

◆ ◆ ◆ ◆ ◆

A Special Club

Here's an idea that might work great. How many other children do you know who are stepchildren? There are probably a bunch around the school or church you attend.

It would be terrific if you and the other stepchildren in your community could get together once in a while and talk about what it's like. Maybe you could help each other understand how to enjoy being a stepchild. You could talk about the good times, the hard things, and the mysteries.

Some groups like this do exist. They don't have to meet year round. They could get together once a week for a few months in the fall or winter or whenever.

Maybe the group could be called:

The Stepladders   The Sidesteps

The Ice Cream Splits   The Split Decision

The Split Heirs   The Split-Level Kids

The Side Splitters   The Double-jointed Kids

The Split Personalities

You can come up with a good name later. For now, talk to your friends about the idea. If two or three seem interested, go to a teacher or a pastor or another adult and ask if he or she would help sponsor the group.

Not only could it be fun, but it might make living in a stepfamily a little bit better.

◆ ◆ ◆ ◆ ◆

Finding Space

Once upon a time there was a family complete with mom, dad, two kids, and a dog named Bruno. For some reason, things either blew up or fizzled out, and the family split with people going their own ways. As time went by, one of the parents found a new love and got married. With marriage came a new parent, a new brother, a new sister, and a cat named Orlando.

With people moving out, people moving in, people moving around, and a dog chasing a cat through the kitchen, it was hard for the kids to find their own space and keep their heads glued on right. Sound familiar?

Adjusting to new people and to new situations can be tough, but it can be done. Usually it takes some extra thoughtfulness, a lot of patience, regular doses of forgiveness, and a fair amount of time.

Try to stay away from snap judgments about people. It takes time to get to know stepbrothers, stepsisters, stepparents, and pet tarantulas. Give everyone a chance. They won't be exactly like you. Their tastes in clothes, music, and videos will probably be different. Their idea of neat or clean or keeping promises might differ, too.

But basically the new people are the same as you. They have the same wants and fears, the same heartaches and hopes. We tend to get along with most people after we get to know them. Try not to judge people—especially when you first meet them.

Getting along is a learnable skill. You could probably live with a lion, but you wouldn't want to step on its tail too often.

Most people appreciate having some space and privacy. Rubbing elbows all the time begins to annoy even the best of friends. It's nice if everyone can have his or her own room, but millions of people share with someone else. Having even part of a closet or a dresser is a big help. The feeling that something is yours and that no one else will look into it is important.

Jesus reminded us of a rule that works well all over the world in all kinds of situations. We call it the Golden Rule, and it explains how we should treat others—even members of a stepfamily: "In everything, do to others what you would have them do to you" (Matthew 7:12a).

◆ ◆ ◆ ◆ ◆

Will This Marriage
Break Up, Too?

Will this marriage break up, too? Probably most children wonder this when their family goes into a second marriage. They have seen one split, and they know it could happen again. What kind of proof is there that this marriage will stick together?

There are no cages where we can lock up a marriage and keep it. There are no magic chains to hold a couple together. We have all learned that families may not be forever.

But the question is worth asking. And the best people to ask are your parent and stepparent. Don't ask them when they don't have time to answer. If necessary, tell them you have an important question and want to know when you can talk to them. Explain that it will take a few minutes to discuss it. If that won't work, simply ask your question at the dinner table, at bedtime, or while they are sitting quietly in the living room or the family room.

What kind of an answer are you looking for? If they say, "Oh, no, we would never break up," you know that is no guarantee, but it is nice to hear. They might tell you how much they care for each other or how good their relationship is or how well they handle disagreements. They may also say that they are asking God for help in their relationship. It helps to hear parents and stepparents say that. By asking your question, you could help everyone. You feel better by saying how you feel. You also let your family know what is going on in your mind. They won't have to guess what you are thinking.

The question may also remind your parent and stepparent that this marriage affects you. That is all the more reason to give the marriage their very best.

◆ ◆ ◆ ◆ ◆

How to Love a Stepperson

Have you ever thought that it isn't fair to make you live with people you don't even know? You didn't choose these people. Someone else made the decision, and now you have to try and get along with a new adult and maybe a new brother or sister and maybe a cat you never met before.

You didn't ask for the divorce or the death, and you may not have asked for the remarriage, but they happened anyway. And now you are supposed to try and get along with everybody.

Have you ever had those thoughts? Tons of children have felt that way.

How do you begin to care for someone you didn't choose to live with? How do you start to love a person who isn't your natural relative? How do you love a stepperson?

You can do it. It happens in most cases. Perhaps in a few situations love may be too much to expect, but it is reasonable for the great majority of people. Love is probably possible with your stepperson.

Love is an action and not a feeling. You can't grit your teeth, tense your muscles, and try to make yourself feel love. If you don't have a mushy, warm, gooey need to be near your stepperson all the time, don't sweat it. That doesn't mean you can't love the person.

You can love a person if you start doing loving things for him or her. If you volunteer to help with the dishes or ask if you can wash the car, you are doing something loving. When you shrink back and have nothing to do with a person, your behavior is unloving.

What would be a loving thing to do for your stepperson?

Could you get the newspaper for him?

Could you take out the trash?

Could you fix dessert?

Could you run an errand for her?

Could you clean off the table?

Could you pick up in the garage?

If you do loving actions, the mushy, warm, gooey feelings might come later. But don't wait for the feelings first. When you eat a candy bar you don't enjoy the taste first and then eat the chocolate. By eating the chocolate you also get the taste. Do loving things and don't sweat the feelings at first.

Jesus taught us that love is an action. He didn't simply feel love for us; he did something. He died on the cross as an act of love.

"Greater love has no one than this, that he lay down his life for his friends" (John 15:13).

New Faces

The day finally arrived. Tim had been dreading this day since he first heard about it. Kent, his new stepbrother, was moving into the room down the hall. He wondered how his mother could do this to him. It was all right for her to marry this new guy; after all, they loved each other. But what a lousy deal it was to have a stepbrother dumped on you when you had no say about it.

When the huge rental truck backed into their driveway, Tim poked his head outside the front door to take a peek. Soon he was hauling boxes into Kent's bedroom. He even began to talk to the newcomer.

Groaning, Tim lowered a large box into one corner of Kent's room. His eye caught the video games that were piled on top. He took a minute to read the labels on a few. Tim was impressed but didn't say anything.

The next box he carried was just sports stuff—a couple of nice looking gloves and a lacrosse stick. He didn't know anybody who owned a lacrosse stick. Tim thought it might be cool to learn how to use one of those.

Kent didn't have a lot of boxes for his room, but what there was caught Tim's attention. Kent had an entire box of games, an oversized skateboard, and some fishing gear. The fishing gear wasn't much, but Tim could think of a few pieces he could give to Kent.

Maybe having a stepbrother wasn't the greatest thing in the world, Tim thought to himself, but it didn't look all bad either. If someone else *had* to move in, he concluded, at least he brought some interesting stuff with him.

Change is usually hard, but most of us are able to make the adjustments. Smart people look for the good and make the most of it. If we fight change, we almost always create problems for ourselves as well as for others.

At first, stepbrothers and stepsisters are strangers, and it takes time to get to know each other. But if we are flexible, loving, and accepting, some strangers become the best of friends.

Jesus said, "I was a stranger and you invited me in" (Matthew 25:35c).

Don't Be a Judge

Would you like to put on a long, black robe and sit behind a large, wooden desk and listen to people argue? Would you like to beat your gavel on the desk and announce whether people were guilty or innocent? It would be up to you to decide who was right and who was wrong.

A judge is helpful in a courtroom. He or she has to make decisions and keep order. But children aren't old enough to be judges, and it isn't fair to ask them to judge other people.

Sometimes parents and stepparents forget that. They ask their children to decide who is right and who is wrong. A parent will tell a child what the other parent has done and then ask, "Do you think that's fair?"

They ask children to act as judges, to pick sides, to say one person is messing up and the other person isn't. No one should ask a child to choose which parent is right or wrong.

Parents do make mistakes. Sometimes they even do things that are terribly bad. But a parent shouldn't use a child to fight the other parent. If the argument is between two parents, it is an adult problem, and a child shouldn't be asked to judge.

The Bible tells us, "Do not judge" (Matthew 7:1a). We don't know everything that was said and done. The adults have enough trouble trying to figure that out. Most children have opinions of what has happened and what is still going on, but that doesn't mean they understand who is right and who is wrong.

When a parent says, "Well, don't you think he or she is wrong?" you might have to answer, "I don't know. It isn't up to me to judge. I just try to love both of you."

◆ ◆ ◆ ◆ ◆

Happier Parents

When my father remarried, he didn't ask me what I thought about it. He made the decision because it was something he wanted to do. He and my stepmother were adults, and they weren't looking for a child to give them advice.

God gave my father and stepmother twenty-five good years together. The marriage changed my father into a happier person. He became more outgoing, became involved in groups, and got along great with my stepmother.

The happiness on their faces made life better for me and for everyone else around them. It wasn't for me to complain or wish they had never met. Their marriage was an adult thing, and it turned out excellently.

All of us are better off with happy parents. When things go well for parents, they usually go better for the children, too. Smart children don't try to fight their parent's new relationship. They never try to come between their parent and their stepparent. When they can, children might offer to help do the dishes or pick up the house so the couple can go on a date or have friends over.

Happiness isn't a contest. Don't think that *either* your parent and stepparent are going to be happy *or* you and your parent are going to be happy. Happiness is usually contagious. If the adults have it, the child is more likely to catch it, too.

Some children become frightened. They believe that their parent's happiness means they might lose their parent. They are afraid that their parent will enjoy being with the stepparent so much that he or she will ignore the child.

They need to lighten up and trust happiness. Normally people who are content make everyone around them feel better, too.

Today you might want to ask God to give your parent an extra dose of peace, joy, love, and contentment. He or she deserves all of that. And so do you.

"A happy heart makes the face cheerful" (Proverbs 15:13).

A Visiting Stepsister

When is a child like a revolving door? When he or she comes into a family for a weekend, goes around in circles for a couple of days, and then spins out and goes back to his or her other family. The child never really settles down or feels at home.

We call these children visiting stepbrothers or stepsisters. Some lead uncomfortable lives as they stand around uneasily in a "foreign" house. But they don't have to feel so uncomfortable. Some planning and thoughtfulness might help them settle into their other "nest" even if it is for just a couple days.

Whether you are the visitor or visitors come to your house, here are a few suggestions to keep in mind:

1. *Work hard to find things in common.*
   Don't insist that everyone play your games, watch your shows, or go to your choice of places.

2. *Help around the house.* Volunteer to help with dishes or invite the visitor to do the dishes with you. Don't jump into major labor like building a garage, but doing everyday jobs together can be important. Involvement makes everyone feel like he or she is part of the group.

3. *Provide some private space.* If a room isn't available, ask for some closet space or drawer space or even a special corner. A shelf in the medicine cabinet can be helpful.

4. *Keep it simple.* Trips to amusement parks are neat, but don't do it too often. You want to get to know each other, and a

large, noisy setting is not the best place to do that.

A good mixture of getting out and of staying home may be the best formula. Food, games, conversations at the table, sharing toys, and doing simple jobs like taking out the trash are people activities. Hurrying everywhere for two days are revolving door activities.

Whether you are the visiting child or there is a child who visits you, keep these guidelines in mind. You will enjoy each other better the more you get to know each other and the more you do together.

Chill Out

Do you ever feel friction in the air? You can tell everyone is uptight. People either stop talking or answer in short, crisp sentences.

It's no fun sitting around a dinner table when people are upset. Maybe someone's feelings have been hurt or something unkind has been said and another person is angry.

That happens in all kinds of families—traditional families, divorced families, and blended families.

54

Often people need to chill out. They need to let their anger cool down and allow the tension to drop below the boiling point. Every family gets too hot sometimes. It's only natural.

When family members become too stiff, there are some moves that might help. If someone says to another family member, "Brenda, why don't we bake cookies?" or "Tony, I'd like to play catch," it might cut the tension.

Brenda and Tony may turn down the invitation, but they might accept it, too. And a move like this might work with a stepparent, a parent, a brother, a sister, a stepbrother, or a stepsister.

Life in a household where no one is talking to anyone else is absolutely no fun. You begin to worry about what the other person is thinking or you try to figure out who is mad at whom. And often the tension has started over some little misunderstanding.

If cookies or catch don't work, think of something else you could do. How about a trip to the park, a walk in the mall, riding bikes, building something, or playing a game?

Sitting and staring can make a tense situation worse. Being active with another family member could help everyone chill out. It isn't your job to make everyone happy, but it does make sense if you make yourself happy and take one other person with you.

When others want to sit around and sulk or steam, that doesn't mean you have to join them. Pick out one or two others and get moving.

A Whiney Engine

The Poston family lived in a nice home with three bedrooms, a bath and a half, and central heat. On a cold winter evening they would often sit home and watch a few good television shows.

Mr. Poston sat in a large chair. Mrs. Poston sat in a larger chair. Ben usually sat on the floor, while Virginia sat on the couch. Benzeen, their goldfish, swam in the aquarium.

During one of those quiet evenings at home, a whiney noise started coming out of the central heating system. Ben asked, "What's that?" Virginia put her hands over her ears, and Mrs. Poston made an ugly face. Benzeen settled on the bottom of the bowl and put his fins over his head.

Mr. Poston hurried to the basement, grabbed a can of oil, and started looking for whatever caused the irritating whine. He worked and squirted and squirted and worked, but the whine didn't go away.

Ben turned up the television to try to drown out the whine. Virginia put on her coat and headed for the neighbors' house. Mrs. Poston retreated to the kitchen and ran water for the dishes. Benzeen pushed his head into the wet sand.

A whining engine is like a whining person. When someone never likes anything, his or her conversation just drones on and on. Before long the people around the whining person turn up the television, leave the house, go to the kitchen, or stick their heads under pillows.

No one enjoys hearing someone whine all the time.

◆ ◆ ◆ ◆ ◆

Cinderella Is Just a Story

Everyone knows the story of Cinderella, the poor young woman who is made a slave to her wicked stepmother and two terrible stepsisters. She has to do all the dirty jobs around the house, and her stepfamily makes fun of her. Her situation becomes so difficult that both a fairy godmother and a handsome prince are needed to rescue her from the miserable stepfamily.

Possibly the best known of all fairy tales, this is a great story. It probably helps many children dream about good things when life is tough. They imagine a knight in shining armor rescuing them or a father-king returning to claim them. It's all fun and exciting, except for one little problem: the story makes stepfamilies look like ugly monsters.

Cinderella is just a story. Stepparents aren't two-headed ghouls. Neither are they superparents. Stepparents can be the finest and most caring people you could imagine. In most cases, they are just normal people. Occasionally they are forgetful and even thoughtless. At other times they are generous, helpful, and extremely kind. That's normal. And normal is all we can hope for from anyone.

Fairy tales like Cinderella or Snow White or Hansel and Gretel show stepparents as mean people instead of simply normal. Because we learn these stories as children, too often we become prejudiced against stepparents. We think they must be awful characters like bank robbers or pirates or drug dealers. As a result, some children dislike stepparents before they even get to know them.

Every stepparent deserves a chance. Don't prejudge your stepparent. Get to know him or her as you would any other person. Look for good qualities and be open to kindness.

Someday you may thank God that your stepparent is a normal person.

◆ ◆ ◆ ◆ ◆

When You Have a Complaint!

As soon as Debbie was inside the front door, her stepfather began yelling.

"Why in the world do you want to hang around with a girl like Tonya?" he barked. "She's always in trouble."

"She isn't. . . ." Debbie started to reply.

"Don't tell me." His face was red. "She's in the principal's office half the time."

"That's not. . . ."

"Her parents can't do anything with her," he interrupted. "Your mother and I don't want to see you with her again. You have enough problems as it is." Slump shouldered, Debbie's stepfather walked away leaving her speechless.

What can Debbie do? She's angry. She doesn't believe Tonya is a bad person, and she thinks most of what her stepfather said is untrue and unfair. How is she going to straighten this out and keep Tonya as her friend?

Every family is different, but some principles are worth keeping in mind.

1. *Talk to the person with whom you have the problem—if at all possible.*

Debbie might look for a time when her step-father is in a better mood. She then might sit down with him and try to explain the situation as she sees it. There is a chance that a calm discussion could change his mind. It's also possible that he might be able to show Debbie a side of Tonya's personality that she doesn't realize.

Talking to the person with whom she has the problem—her stepfather—is almost always the best route. If Debbie goes immediately to her mother to gripe about her stepfather, she may hurt everyone's relationship. He might think the two of them are teaming up against him.

It doesn't help communication to go around someone. You show respect if you try to work it out with the person.

2. *But what if there is absolutely no way to talk with a stepparent or a parent?*

If you absolutely can't talk to your stepparent, then go to the parent you *can* talk to.

Breakdown in communication does happen, although not as often as you might think. If you have tried to talk to the person, and if the situation is unfair and must be changed, *go to the parent with whom you are most comfortable.* You need to talk to someone. You can't keep swallowing your feelings.

Communication is tricky, and you don't want to complain all the time, but real problems need to be handled. Since Debbie is bothered by her stepfather's decision, she needs to talk to him or to her mother.

◆ ◆ ◆ ◆ ◆

The Piano Recital

Candice didn't look nervous when she walked to the piano, but she thought her knees were going to give way. She smiled at the audience and sat down to play. Afraid to look around, Candice didn't want to look at her mother who sat on the left side of the room or at her father who sat on the right side.

She tried not to play too rapidly. After two years of lessons, the fifth grader knew how important pacing and timing were. Her stepmother had often reminded her to slow down and follow the music.

Halfway through, Candice wondered what her piano teacher was thinking. She was an excellent teacher, Candice thought, patient and kind. Every week she was in a good mood and gave Candice's stepmother a cup of coffee while she waited to give her a ride home.

Candice finished the piece and briskly stood up to take a short bow. She loved the applause and remembered how pretty she felt in her new, light green dress. Her stepmother had taken her to pick out the material and had spent long hours sewing to get it ready in time.

After the recital was over, Candice hurried toward her mother, whom she hadn't seen for months. Her mother's broad smile showed how proud she was of her talented daughter.

Almost as quickly Candice crossed the aisle and hugged her father. He told her how pretty she looked and what a great job she had done.

Taking her mother by one hand and her father by the other, she pulled her reluctant parents toward the next room to get cookies and punch. It was one of the proudest days in young Candice's life.

Meanwhile her stepmother stood alone and waited until the reception was over.

Does Your Stepparent Love You?

When someone new comes into your world, you are bound to have questions about your relationship. Will the two of you be close, or will you have trouble understanding each other? Will you enjoy being together, or will you argue over the bathroom, homework, and whether or not you watch crazy TV shows?

Underneath all these questions is this one: Will my stepparent love me, or will he or she be the creature from the deep lagoon?

It would be easy to dismiss a question like this and simply answer, "Of course your stepparent loves you. Don't give it another thought." But children are smarter than that. They know that some stepparents do not love their stepchildren just as some stepchildren don't love their stepparents.

No book can tell you whether or not your new parent will love you. But it can offer some advice on how to make love grow:

1. *Don't expect your stepparent to love you deeply the first time you meet.* He or she might like you, but real love usually comes slowly. Love must grow; it doesn't arrive in full bloom. Get to know each other. Take your relationship a step at a time. Ask God to help you along the way.

2. *Love attracts love.* Try to love your stepparent. That may take time, too. The work of love begins with you and not with someone else. How can you grow in love for the new person?

3. *Show respect.* Kindness and politeness can come instantly. We can show respect for a total stranger. Treat your stepparent with thoughtfulness and consideration. It will go a long way toward building a loving relationship.

4. *Look for show and tell.* Can you see acts of love? Does your stepparent find ways to

help you, play with you, listen to you? Sometimes people show us in many ways that they love us, yet we still don't believe them. Others say they love us and treat us like dust balls. The biggest proof of love is action. You don't expect the person to sing you a love song, but you appreciate it when someone shows that he or she cares.

Don't ask for instant love. Slowly grow in your love for each other. "Love is patient, love is kind" (1 Corinthians 13:4a).

Talking To a Brick Wall

Have you ever had the feeling that you were talking but no one was listening? You were saying the words, explaining your problems, but no one seemed to understand? And you knew it wasn't your fault. You weren't keeping it all inside or clamming up or hiding from everybody. You were up-front, straightforward, communicating, and no one seemed to care about what you were saying.

That's when you feel like you are talking to a brick wall.

And you might be. That person might listen all day and still not have a clue as to what you mean or how you feel. Soon you become frustrated and even angry. And sometimes you can't even get anyone to listen to you in the first place.

No matter how frustrated you feel, don't clam up. If you stop talking and stop trying, your situation could get worse.

If you feel like there is a brick wall at home, find someone else to talk to. It wouldn't be as though you were running off to tell stories about your family. If you are bothered by something or if you have a problem you can't solve, you could get some tremendous help by talking to someone else.

Who can you talk to?

a grandparent
a teacher
a friend
a counselor
a neighbor
a minister
a youth worker
God

Do you have a cookie person (not a cookie monster)? A cookie person is someone special who makes you feel good when you talk to him or her. A cookie person may or may not have any real cookies, but you feel comfortable talking to that person.

After you talk to someone else, you may be able to go back home and explain what you were trying to say before. And this time you might not find a brick wall.

◆ ◆ ◆ ◆ ◆

Our Superparent

How many parents do you have? You might have a parent and a stepparent. You also might have another parent and another stepparent. In some cases a parent remarries a third time. Then you have a parent, a former stepparent, and another stepparent. It's enough to make your head swim.

Then, of course, there are grandparents. Usually there are four grandparents. But your stepparent also has parents. They aren't exactly grandparents, but they are nice people.

There are so many parents that a child would get dizzy trying to keep track of them all.

No one wants to add to the confusion, but there is still another parent to keep in mind. This parent isn't like any of the others. This one is more like Superparent. The extra parent we sometimes forget about is God.

The Bible tells us, "How great is the love the Father has lavished on us, that we should be called children of God!" (1 John 3:1).

All of us realize that families can change. People might move away, get divorced, stop talking to a family member, stop loving each other, or die—all sorts of stress and upheaval can happen. None of that goes on between us and our Parent in heaven. We have a steady, immovable relationship with our Superparent.

Our Superparent lavishes love on us. Lavish means love is poured on us like water from a shower. God loves us completely and at all times.

God sent his Son to live and die for us. That is a large part of God's love. By believing in Jesus Christ we receive the love of God.

Superparent cares for us every day and enjoys having us in his family—forever.

◆ ◆ ◆ ◆ ◆

What Happened in the First Marriage?

Almost every Sunday afternoon Ann Marie used to go over to Donna's house and they would do things together. Sometimes they would make cookies while they listened to tapes. Other times they would walk down to the drive-in and get a soft drink while they talked about everything and yet about nothing.

At first Ann Marie wanted to go to Donna's house every week. They had a special friendship. After a month, Ann Marie noticed that Donna had some irritating habits. Often she demanded her own way. Ann Marie didn't get to pick out the tapes. She also noticed that Donna liked to talk all the time. If Ann Marie was telling a story, Donna would jump in and start talking before Ann Marie was finished. That really ticked Ann Marie.

After a couple of months, Ann Marie began going over to Donna's house less and less. By the time school started that fall, she had stopped going altogether.

Many times two friends get along extremely well for a while and then start to pull apart. It would be good if they could discuss their differences and stay friends, but that doesn't always work. The same is true for married couples. At first they seem to really enjoy being with each other, but then some husbands and wives can't deal with their problems and differences.

There are many reasons why some couples don't get along:

They might argue too much.

They might be bored with each other.

They might not talk enough.

They might have different interests.

They might drink too much or use drugs.

They might be terrible at handling money.

They might not be able to solve problems.

They might have found someone else.

At the same time, there are millions of married couples who love each other for 25, 30, 40, or more years. Marriages can work and are often very happy.

It is difficult to say why a marriage breaks up. Sometimes the couple doesn't understand why they couldn't make it work.

The best way to find out what happened to your parents' marriage is to ask them. It is important that you know as much as you can. Don't be pushy or demanding, but ask them this simple question: "Why didn't you two stay married?" They may be looking for the opportunity to explain that to you.

Love Isn't a Hat

Suppose you have a bright orange hat that a lot of people like. They like it so much that they want to wear it. Because you are generous, you loan your hat to your brother, to your sister, and to Festus, the paperboy.

Since you have only one hat, you can loan it to only one person at a time. When that person is done with the hat, you have to get it back and then loan it to someone else.

You're a nice person, and you don't mind sharing, but you obviously can't loan your hat to four or six or eight people all at once.

You also have something called love. Love means that you care and are kind and that you help people. Most of us grew up loving two parents. We didn't have to learn that, because love for parents comes fairly naturally.

Because of divorce or death and remarriage, your family became complicated. Instead of two parents, there are now three or four parents and maybe more. The numbers have grown, and you might be trying to figure out whom to love.

If you love your stepfather, do you have to love your father less? If you love your step-mother, will your mother think you don't love her? What if your mother and father don't like each other? Do you have to stop loving one of them because they fight each other? How can you give love to so many people? How can you love two people who don't love each other?

Fortunately, love isn't a hat. You can give your hat to only one person at a time. But love is something you can share with one, two, or ten people all at once. You don't have to take love back before you can give it to someone else. You can keep loving the person you know while you begin to love a new person. There is plenty of love to go around.

You don't need to feel guilty because you love two or four or six parents. You can love half a dozen or more brothers and sisters. You never have to take love away from one person in order to give it to someone else.

"I hear about your faith in the Lord Jesus and your love for all the saints" (Philemon 5).

◆ ◆ ◆ ◆ ◆

Parent Stealing

No matter what the circumstances, when one parent moves away, that is hard to deal with. A family is the most important group a person can belong to. A church or a club can mean a great deal, but parents are flesh and blood. No one can ever take the place of a parent.

When one parent is gone, there is only one left. Anyone who has lost a parent has gone through terrible pain and confusion. The person may even worry about losing the second parent.

It may be that while you are still trying to get over the loss of one parent, a new person has come into your life. That person started dating and then became engaged to the only parent you had left. Maybe you are beginning to wonder if this new person is going to steal the only parent you have left. It's not likely that you think the new person will physically carry off your mom or dad. But you may think that because of the new person, your mom or dad will love you less.

In my family that wasn't true. When my father remarried, his new wife only made life better for everyone. My father was happier, and his happiness made everything better for me.

Many children worry about parent stealing, and often parents have no idea that it bothers the child. This is where children need to help out. Children need to be straightforward and say something like: "You aren't going to leave me, too, are you?" "If you love him, will you still love me?" "Will you still have time to take me shopping on Saturdays?"

However it's said, parents need to know what children are thinking. You should never expect your parent to guess how you feel. Parental love is too important to worry about. No child wants a parent's love stolen away.

Stirring Up Trouble

Whenever Christy visited her father's house, she liked to talk about her stepfather. She noticed that if she would tell her dad what she didn't like about her stepfather, her father would become extremely interested.

Christy didn't have any big complaints. Her stepfather didn't abuse her or anything like that. She simply mentioned his faults or bad habits.

"Dan keeps the TV on during dinner time," Christy said of her stepfather.

"That's no way to run a family," her father would reply. "How are you guys ever going to communicate with that thing blaring?"

Christy enjoyed it. She liked to put her stepfather down. She also wanted her father to agree that Dan was a dud. Her father encouraged her to tell him more. He wanted to know he was a better father than Dan.

"You wouldn't believe what Dan does," she continued. "If he loses at basketball, he pouts. Boy, you'd think he has to win at everything."

"I hate to say this," her father added, "but sometimes you must wonder how mature Dan really is."

No big complaints. Just gossipy little tidbits. By talking about them Christy felt closer to her father. In turn, her father encouraged her because it made him sound like a better father than Dan.

Talking and sharing are important. None of us should clam up and keep everything inside. But we shouldn't tell meaningless little stories just to hurt people. Gossip is wrong whether in traditional families or stepfamilies.

Some children like to play their parents against each other. And some parents like to dig up juicy tales about the other parent. When they do, they are trying to stir up trouble.

Smart people don't get caught in the middle. If parents want to needle one another, they shouldn't use their children to do it. Gossip is interesting and exciting, but it's also harmful and mean.

"The words of a gossip are like choice morsels; they go down to a man's inmost parts" (Proverbs 18:8).

74

◆ ◆ ◆ ◆ ◆

But What If . . . ?

A few stepparents *are* abusive to their stepchildren. Some children are verbally, physically, or sexually abused.

If that happens, the child should go and tell his or her parent *immediately.*

There are people who can help you. Ministers, teachers, and counselors can step in for you. But if at all possible go to your parent first and see if he or she can help.

◆ ◆ ◆ ◆ ◆

What About Stepgrandparents?

Do you have a favorite dessert? You know, the hot fudge sundae that tops off a burger and fries. Or maybe that slice of creme pie that slides down so easily, making a great meal even better. Desserts are like that. Even though you could do without them, it's nice to have that little extra "something."

If a stepfamily were a meal, then the scrumptious dessert, that extra "something," might be stepgrandparents. They are the parents of your stepfather or stepmother. They aren't your blood, or biological, relatives, but you may be in contact with them from time to time. Stepgrandparents are more like older friends. Their grown child is your stepparent, so you have something in common on the first day you meet. With more contacts you may discover that you like to do things together.

Discuss with your parents what to call your stepgrandparents, because you need to call them something. People get along better if they are comfortable with their names for each other.

Stepgrandparents may not see you often. That doesn't mean they don't like you. Other stepgrandparents may live closer, and you might get to know them better. They aren't usually part of the meal, but if it works out, they can be great desserts.

◆ ◆ ◆ ◆ ◆

Immovable Objects

A girl was out hiking in the woods one summer afternoon. As she broke through into a clearing, she came upon a rock as large as a small house. The rock was not blocking the trail; the path went around, but the girl became upset. "What a lousy deal," she thought. "That's no place for a big, ugly rock. It messes up the trail."

The more she looked at the rock, the angrier she became. She spit at the rock. She called it names. Eventually she sat down and folded her arms over her face and cried.

It's a silly story, isn't it? What young person would behave in such a stupid way? Why doesn't the girl think it through and find some way to live with the rock? The path leads around the rock, so why doesn't she simply keep going? She knows that she can spit and gripe and cry all day, but the rock is not going to roll away for her.

Sometimes we are like the girl and the rock. We get angry about things we can't change, and we do dumb things. We aren't stupid, but we act that way.

It may be that we get a teacher we don't like and therefore refuse to try and get along with him. Or our parents don't give us enough money, so we treat them rudely. Or our friends don't want to play our game, so we walk off and go home.

Stepfamilies have rocks, too. Something gets in the path. A stepbrother moves in. A stepsister comes to visit twice a month. A father hardly ever calls. The family moves to another neighborhood. Those are the large rocks in the trail of our lives.

Sometimes we want to spit, gripe, cry, or do all three. But why should we get bent out of shape over things we cannot change? If we kick the rock, we get a sore foot. If we push against the rock, we get a sore shoulder.

Smart people learn to live with the things they can't change. They ask God to help them have a good attitude. If you beat your head against a rock, you only get a big headache. And the rock doesn't even budge.

The things you cannot change you learn to accept and live with. After a while you may barely notice the rock anymore.

◆ ◆ ◆ ◆ ◆

Snow White's Jealous Stepmother

An old fairy tale tells of a stepmother who would stand in front of a mirror and say, "Mirror, mirror, on the wall, who's the fairest of them all?"

Each time the magic mirror answered that the self-centered stepmother was the best-looking woman in the land. But as the years went by, her stepdaughter, Snow White, grew up and increased in beauty.

One day the stepmother asked her mirror the usual question, but she didn't get the usual answer. This time she was told that Snow White was now at the top of the beauty list.

Furious, the jealous stepmother had Snow White thrown out of the palace.

The story of Snow White shows us how mean and ugly jealousy can be. Jealousy happens when we are only interested in ourselves, and we fall into the foolish habit of constantly comparing ourselves with other people. We are not satisfied with being who we are. We have to be better than everyone else. And usually we think that others are getting the breaks.

Jealousy is extremely harmful. By comparing ourselves, we make it hard to simply enjoy who we are.

When a stepparent enters a family, some children may become jealous. That's easy to understand. The new person takes up more of the parent's time and more of his or her affection.

As we see in the Snow White story, the stepparent can also become jealous of the child. That jealousy can lead people to say and do some very painful things.

Your parent's new spouse is important to your parent. You are also important to him or her. Stepparents and children don't need to be in competition with each other. Each person fills his or her own place in the family. Stepparents can never take the place of children, and children can never take the place of stepparents.

It would be as if a helicopter was jealous of an airplane. Why should they worry over which is best? Each is important in its own special way. The worst thing they could do is to get jealous and start crashing into each other.

Snow White's stepmother could have been happy with herself and with her stepdaughter. No one needed to get jealous.

"Anger is cruel and fury overwhelming, but who can stand before jealousy?" (Proverbs 27:4).

◆ ◆ ◆ ◆ ◆

Should Marcie Be Adopted?

After two years of living with her stepfather and her natural mother, Marcie was asked to make a big decision. Her natural father had almost no contact with her. Sometimes she would get a birthday card, or she might get a phone call but only when he had been drinking heavily. He acted like he felt guilty about not having her but did little to show he cared.

The decision Marcie was asked to make was whether or not she would like to be adopted. At first Marcie was confused. She thought only babies were adopted. Her stepfather and mother explained the details carefully.

If she wanted to be adopted, they would apply to the court. If the court agreed to the adoption, several things would happen.

1. Marcie would become legally and officially adopted. Her stepfather would then become her legal father.

2. Her natural father would no longer have any control over Marcie. He would not support her financially, and he couldn't

tell her or her mother or her new father what to do. He would give up Marcie.

3. Marcie's last name would be changed to the same as her stepfather.

Sometimes adoptions are easy, and the natural parent agrees to it immediately. Other times parents fight the adoption in court. No one could predict what Marcie's father would do.

Marcie's decision would be even harder if she felt that her father loved her and wanted to be near her. She didn't feel that way because he never came around.

Yet the decision would not be easy. Marcie would need time to think it over. She would probably come back later and ask more questions.

What do you think Marcie should do?

They're Having a Baby

Normally this would be happy news. Your parents are going to have a child. A new brother or sister is going to come wiggling into your family. There will be loads of happiness complete with presents, rattles, crying, and messy diapers.

Everyone is in for plenty of excitement and lots of commotion.

If all those good things are going to happen, why do you feel left out and lonely? Why aren't you jumping up and down with joy? Maybe the reason is because your parents aren't having the baby; instead your parent and stepparent are bringing this one into the world.

Will another child, with a different parent involved, pull your natural parent away from you? Do you see a second family, like a mini-family, forming, one of which you won't be a part? Those are the kinds of fears that bother many children when a baby shows up. In a step-family the children may even have a few extra questions.

Don't hesitate to tell your parents what you think. Take time to ask what is going on and what kind of changes might take place. You need to know, and your parents might not think to tell you. Where will the baby sleep? Where will the baby sit at the table? Where will the baby ride in the car?

When you talk to your parents, remember some important facts:

1. *No one can take your place.* There is only one you. Don't be jealous of a new baby; children can't replace children.

2. *The baby will need you.* Ask your parents how you can help. Can you rock the baby, feed him or her, maybe baby-sit? There is a great deal of work, and your parents will be glad to know you are available.

3. *Love never runs out.* If you have a bucket of paint and you paint a house, the bucket will soon be empty. Love isn't a bucket of paint, and it doesn't run out. Parents can paint a child with love and also paint a second child. In the next minute they can turn around and paint two more.

Parents have enough love to paint all the children over and over again.

"All the special gifts and powers from God will someday come to an end, but love goes on forever" (1 Corinthians 13:8 LB).

◆ ◆ ◆ ◆ ◆

Why Do Adults
Go Away Alone?

Ten-year-old Jody was grumbling around the house. She could understand why Mrs. Newberry had to baby-sit her younger brother and sister, but she didn't want anyone telling her what to do. Besides, Jody told herself, she was old enough to do some baby-sitting herself.

Jody wondered why her mother and stepfather had to go out anyway. They were just trying to get away from the children, she thought. The adults would go on weekend holidays and sometimes go away for a whole week without the children. She was sure they could hardly wait to get rid of the kids.

Children in traditional families and children in stepfamilies both wonder about that. Why do parents go off alone and leave the children at home? Don't they like the children?

We can find the answer if we turn the question around. Why do children like to spend the night at someone else's house? Why do children like slumber parties, weekend retreats, and camps? Are the children trying to get rid of their parents because they don't like them?

Try another question. Are there times when you like to get away from your best friend? Do you need a little space, a little change, different scenery? That doesn't mean you have given up on the friend. Later you will come back together and continue to have a great time.

We can spend too much energy wondering if people like us. We want to know why they didn't sit at our table or why they didn't drop by our house or even why we weren't invited to their party. Most of us worry about those kinds of things. But when we stop and think, we realize how silly that can become.

A friend doesn't have to be around all the time. Parents don't have to sit next to us on the couch every evening. If we get away from each other now and then, we will probably have even more fun when we come back together.

The next time the adults go away, give them a giant farewell hug. Getting away is a loving thing to do.

Good and Mad

Every summer Roger liked to play on the lawn in his bare feet. His parents warned him that if he didn't keep his shoes on, he was going to stub a toe or step on a piece of glass or something. Roger ignored his parents and left the house barefooted as often as he could get away with it.

Early one morning, while chasing his dog, Roger let out a horrible yell. Immediately he sat down and grabbed his foot. Roger could feel an awful pain under the small toe on his left foot. He poked around but couldn't find anything. "Must be a sliver," Roger grumbled to himself.

As he walked into the house, Roger tried to keep his feet flat. He didn't want to let his parents know what had happened.

Quickly Roger went to his room and tried to find the tiny piece of glass. Finally, unable to remove the sliver, he put his socks and shoes on and tried to ignore his problem.

But the pain didn't go away. Each step he took caused a sharp pain in his left foot, like a pin prick. After hobbling around for two days, Roger went to his parents and asked them for help.

Many children in stepfamilies are angry. It's like Roger's pain in the foot. They might be angry because of a divorce, a death, the remarriage, the move to a new house, the invasion of stepbrothers or stepsisters, the way they are treated, or for other reasons. They hobble around upset and fuming inside, but they don't want to tell anyone they are mad. They keep it hidden as if they were putting a sock and a shoe over it.

It's good to control anger. You don't want to throw lamps or punch people. But if you just hide your anger, you can't remove it. Hitting people isn't a great idea, and neither is putting a sock over it.

In order for Roger to find help, he had to begin by telling someone. That is also a good way to take care of anger. Tell someone, "I'm really angry. And you know why I'm angry?" Then explain it to the person.

If you can say what makes you angry, you can take the first step toward removing the piece of glass.

◆ ◆ ◆ ◆ ◆

Keeping in Touch
with Grandparents

Have you ever played a video game with too many moving objects? You are trying to keep track of eight pieces on the screen and suddenly you realize that you forgot one of them. That doesn't mean the piece you forgot wasn't important. There was too much to watch.

Too often grandparents are the forgotten pieces. When a family divorces and moves and remarries and goes through many changes, grandparents can get left out of the picture. This is especially true if they are the parents of the parent who moved away. You are most likely to lose contact with that grandmother or grandfather.

They may have been special people in your life. They may have sent gifts or letters. Maybe they visited and did things with you. But because of the upheaval and turmoil in the family, they became the lost people.

That doesn't mean you don't love each other. It simply means they got left out in all the commotion.

If you want to remain close to a grandparent, you need to say so. You need to speak up and let everyone know you want to keep contact with your grandparents. Let them know that you want to visit, you want to write, you want to call.

If your grandparents live far away, tapes are a great idea. You can record letters to them, and they can do the same for you. It's a fun way to share stories, jokes, even songs.

Pictures are another good idea. People like to see each other. Grandparents especially like to know how their grandchildren are growing up. If you have a video camera and they have a VCR, try making a movie for them. Pack it in popcorn!

A diary is another way to keep contact. Each day keep a record of what is going on, and at the end of the week put it in the mail.

Be creative and be personal. Grandparents are terrific people.

The Broken Chair

Her favorite television show was "My Sister the Robot." Amy turned on the set as she did every Thursday evening and grabbed a wooden chair. The theme song rang out as Amy sat down and rocked back on two legs, as she did every week.

SMASH! The chair collapsed backwards, dumping the twelve-year-old on the floor. Amy screamed with pain as the broken chair leg cut through her jeans and tore an ugly gash in her right thigh. Quickly her hand reached the wound and she could feel blood pouring out.

"Mom!" she cried, "Come here!"

Amy survived this painful accident and lived to watch "My Sister the Robot" many more times, but something changed about Amy: she began to look at chairs a bit differently than before.

For a while she sat on the floor. If Amy used a chair, she often tested it first. She would push down on it to see if the chair could hold her weight. And, of course, it was months before she dared lean back on one again.

Once you are hurt by a chair, it can take a while before you will totally trust one again. But you will learn to sit on chairs again if you keep trying.

When a stepparent comes into a family, some children hold back at first. They trusted their parent and that parent is now gone. It takes some time to know if they can trust this new person. The children will want to test the stepparent. Does the person keep her word; does he show love; is she caring? Will the stepparent stay, or will he be there a month and then take off? A new stepparent raises a list of questions.

Slowly, children will lean on the stepparent. They may decide to trust the new person a little, like sitting on the edge of a chair; later they might put more of their weight on the person.

Some children don't wait. They trust the stepparent on the first day. But the children who have been hurt more are often cautious about trusting again.

Once our trust has been hurt, we might have trouble sitting in a chair again. But children are tough and courageous. They learn to come back and trust people.